CW00727515

POCKET
VERY SILLY Jokes

3303484322

OXFORDSHIRE LIBRARY SERVICE

3303484322	
Askews & Holts	28-May-2019
J828.92	£4.99

ARCTURUS

This edition published in 2019 by Arcturus Publishing Limited
26/27 Bickels Yard, 151–153 Bermondsey Street,
London SE1 3HA

Copyright © Arcturus Holdings Limited

All rights reserved. No part of this publication may be reproduced,
stored in a retrieval system, or transmitted, in any form or by any means,
electronic, mechanical, photocopying, recording or otherwise, without
prior written permission in accordance with the provisions of the
Copyright Act 1956 (as amended). Any person or persons who do any
unauthorised act in relation to this publication may be liable to criminal
prosecution and civil claims for damages.

Illustrated by: Fabio Santomauro
Cover illustrated by: Garbiele Tafuni
Designed by: Duck Egg Blue

ISBN: 978-1-78888-730-4
CH006912NT
Supplier 29, Date 0319, Print run 7998

Printed in China

Contents

Animal Antics

Why did the lion eat the stilt walker?

It wanted a well-balanced meal!

What does an octopus use to cut something in half?

A sea-saw!

What do you call a monkey with a scar and a wand?

Hairy Potter!

What do polar bears do when they're not hunting?

They just chill!

What did the frog say when it saw the toad?

Wart's new?

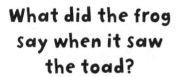

How do you start a firefly race?

On your marks, get set, glow!

What weighs 10 tons and squirts custard at you?

An elephant eating a donut!

Where do sharks go for the winter?

Finland!

What's worse than a bull in a china shop?

A porcupine in a balloon factory!

Why didn't the penguin get married?

Because it got cold feet!

What's big, furry, and flies?

A hot-air baboon!

What's the best job for a spider?

Web designer!

What do you get if you cross a snake with a builder?

A boa constructor!

How does a hippo get to school?

On the hippopotabus!

Why don't tuna play tennis?

They don't want to get caught in the net!

Did you hear the joke about skunks?
No?
Good, because it stunk!

What do you call a man who lives with a pack of wolves?

Wolfgang.

What toy did the baby snake have?

A rattle!

What do you call a flying skunk? A smellycopter!

What did the lobster say to her husband?

Stop being so snappy!

Why are elephants always late for the plane?

Because they take so long to pack their trunks!

What's the fastest way for a reindeer to travel?

By icicle!

What do you call a hairdressing competition for lions?

The mane event!

What did the macaw say to the toucan?

Talk is cheep!

What did the TV presenter say when he saw a herd of wildebeest coming over the hill?

And now for some gnus...

What has 99 legs and one eye?

A pirate centipede!

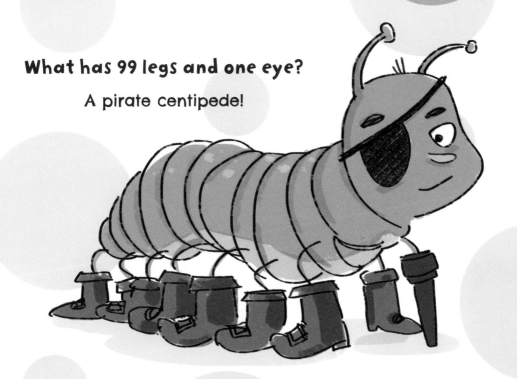

What do you call a really, really old ant?

An antique!

What do you call twin porcupines?

A prickly pair!

What do you get if you spill birdseed in your shoes?

Pigeon toes!

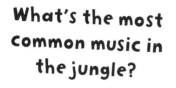

What's the most common music in the jungle?

Snake, rattle, and roll!

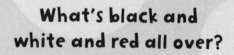

What's black and white and red all over?

A sunburned zebra!

What do you call an empty bowl of parrot food?

Polly-gone!

Which fish do builders like best?

Hammerhead sharks!

What do cheetahs eat?

Fast food!

What did the lion say as it watched the bike race?

Meals on wheels!

What weighs a ton and floats gracefully through the air?

A hang-gliding rhinoceros!

Which jungle creature tells the best jokes?

A stand-up chameleon!

How do apes make cheese sandwiches?

They gorilla them!

Crazy Kitchen

Waiter, there's a twig in my meal!

Just a moment, sir, I'll get the branch manager.

What's small, round, white, and giggles?

A tickled onion!

What did the fast tomato say to the slow tomato?

Come on, ketchup!

Why did the turkey join a band?

He had his own drumsticks!

What's the worst thing about being an octopus?

Washing your hands before dinner.

Did you hear about the banana that went to charm school?

He turned into a real smoothie!

Which drink do frogs enjoy?

Croak-a-cola!

What did the cannibal order at the restaurant?

Pizza with everyone on it!

What do you call a peanut in space?

An astro-nut!

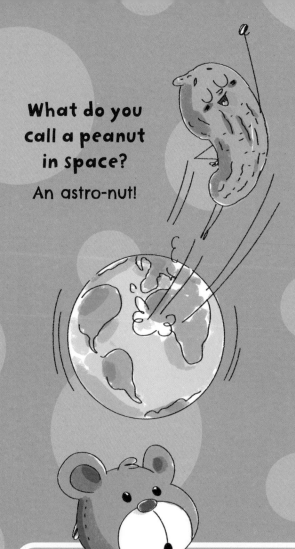

What do you get if you put three ducks in a box?

A box of quackers!

Why couldn't the teddy bear finish its lunch?

Because it was stuffed!

What pizza topping
do anteaters
like best?

Ant-chovies!

How do you fit
an elephant in
the fridge?

Open the door,
and push it
really hard!

What can you serve
but never eat?

Tennis balls!

What do you call a
really large pumpkin?

A plumpkin!

What kind of cheese do you use to lure a bear away?

Camembert! ("Come on bear!")

How do you make golden soup?

Put 24 carrots in it!

Waiter, there are flies in my soup!

Yes, sir, I think it's the rotten meat that attracts them.

What do you get if you cross a pig and a dinosaur?

Jurassic Pork!

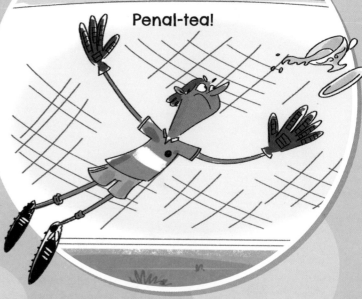

What drink do soccer players like least?

Penal-tea!

What did the nut say when it had a cold?

Cashew!

Where do milkshakes come from?

Dancing cows!

Did you hear about the numbskull who ate a light bulb?

He said he only wanted a light meal.

What kind of key opens a banana?

A mon-key!

Why did the potato cry?

Someone had hurt its peelings!

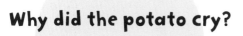

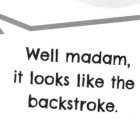

Waiter, what is this fly doing in my soup?

Well madam, it looks like the backstroke.

What are large, have horns, and give milk?

Dairy trucks!

What did the caveman order for lunch?

A club sandwich!

Why won't you starve on a desert island?

Because of the sand which is there (sandwiches there).

Waiter, do you have frog's legs?

No, madam, I always walk like this.

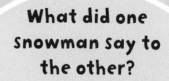

What did one snowman say to the other?

Can you smell carrots?

What do you get if you cross a snake and an apple tart?

A pie-thon!

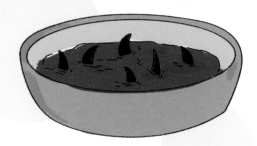

What's red and dangerous?

Shark-infested tomato soup!

Are carrots really good for your eyesight?

Well, have you ever seen a rabbit wearing glasses?

Waiter, why are there morsels of French cheese splattered all over the floor?

It's de Brie, sir.

What do vegetarian spiders eat?

Corn on the cobweb!

What is yellow, sweet, and found in the jungle?

Tarzipan!

Mad Monsters

How can you tell if a skeleton owns an umbrella?

It's bone dry!

Why does Dracula wear lace-up shoes?

Because flip-flops look stupid with his tuxedo!

What kind of music do mummies like?

Wrap music!

Why did the monster stop biting his nails?

His mother said they might be rusty!

Who's the most important player on a monster soccer team?

The ghoul keeper!

What does a witch say when she's made a cauldron full of eyeball soup?

That should see me through the week!

What kind of blood do pessimistic vampires like best?

B negative!

What's big and ugly and blue?

A monster holding its breath!

Where do clever aliens study?

In a parallel university!

Why should you be especially afraid of a vampire dog?

Its bite is worse than its bark!

What goes "ha ha, thunk?"

A monster laughing its head off!

What kind of books do ghosts read?

Whoooo-dunnits!

Why should you never lie to a monster with x-ray vision?

Because it can see right through you!

What is a zombie most likely to receive a medal for?

Dead-ication!

What do you call a werewolf with no money?

Paw!

How did the monster spike its hair?

With scare gel!

What do you call a witch at the seaside?

A sand-witch!

Why can't skeletons play hymns in church?

Because they don't have any organs!

How do you get a baby alien to sleep?

Rocket!

What happens if a green dragon paddles in the Red Sea?

It gets its feet wet!

What game do zombies like playing?

Hide-and-shriek!

What does an ogre drive?

A monster truck!

How do mummies hide?

They wear masking tape!

Which monster has one eye and one wheel?

A unicyclops!

What do ghosts like to eat for dessert?

I scream!

Which meal do sea monsters like best?

Fish and ships!

Which holiday do vampires like best?

Fangs-giving!

What do you call an alien with no eye?

"Alen."

What's black and white and dead all over?

A zombie in a tuxedo!

What do little vampires eat?

Alpha-bat soup!

Why was the monster top of the class?

Because two heads are better than one!

Which monster never uses deodorant?

Stankenstein!

What do you call a
monster in a toy car?

Stuck!

Why do you never
see a fat vampire?

Because they eat
necks to nothing!

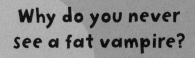

What does a zombie read
first in the newspaper?

Its horror-scope!

Silly School

Which subject do pirates like best?

Arrrrt!

Teacher: Have you put clean water in the fish tank?

Bradley: No, it hasn't drunk the first tankful yet!

Why did the mathematics teacher have an old-fashioned alarm clock?

She liked arithma-ticks!

Which subject do snakes like best?

Hiss-tory!

Teacher: Mike, your ideas are like diamonds.

Mike: What, they are beautiful and precious?

Teacher: No, they're extremely rare!

What did one raindrop Say to the other?

Two's company, three's a cloud!

Science teacher: What happens if you put oxygen with magnesium?

Hannah: OMg!

Coach: Why didn't you stop the ball?

Goalkeeper: I thought that's what the net was for!

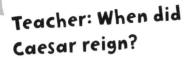

Teacher: When did Caesar reign?

Billy: I didn't know he rained. I thought it was "Hail, Caesar."

What happens if you throw a pile of books into the ocean?

You get a title wave!

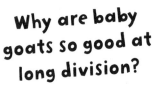

Teacher: If I had 6 apples in one hand and 8 apples in the other, what would I have?

Sally: Enormous hands!

Did you hear about the unhappy algebra book?

It had too many problems.

What is a butterfly's best subject?

Moth-ematics!

What's purple and 5,000 miles long?

The Grape Wall of China!

Miss Addison: Michelle, are those new glasses?

Michelle: Yes, I'm hoping they'll improve di-vision!

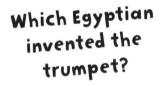

Which Egyptian invented the trumpet?

Tooting-khamun!

Why did the science teacher remove his doorbell?

He wanted to win the no-bell prize!

Teacher: Which of King Arthur's knights invented the round table?

Hailey: Sir Cumference?

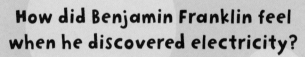

How did Benjamin Franklin feel when he discovered electricity?

Shocked!

What do a burger and a high school teacher have in common?

They're both pro-teen!

Which game do tornadoes like best?

Twister!

Why was the
skeleton kept back a year?

Because it was a numbskull!

What fish does a music
teacher like the best?

A piano tuna!

Why did the
teacher write on
the window?

Because she
wanted her lesson
to be clear.

Did you hear about
the pencil with an
eraser on each end?

It's pointless!

What do you get when you divide the circumference of a jack-o'-lantern by its diameter?

Pumpkin pi!

Why was the student like a seahorse?

His grades were all below C-level.

Teacher: Which was the first animal in space?

Louis: The cow that jumped over the Moon?

Teacher: What kind of creature is that?

Connor: It's our pet, Tiny.

Teacher: But it's so small. What animal is it?

Connor: It's my-newt!

Why did the astronaut walk out of class?

It was launch time!

What was carved on a knight's grave if he died in battle?

Rust in peace!

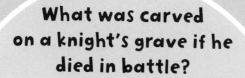

Why was the broom late for school?

It overswept!

Why did the boy eat his homework?

His teacher said it was a piece of cake!

Why did the geometry teacher stay home from class?

She'd sprained her angle!

Where do vampire teachers come from?

Teacher-draining school!

Where did medieval knights park their camels?

In Camelot!

What kind of bus takes you through school, not to school?

A sylla-bus!

Outrageous Outer Space

How do you know
Saturn is married?

You can see its ring!

How do you organize
a space party?

You planet!

Why would an alien rather eat a shooting star than an asteroid?

It's a little meteor!

Did you hear that Albert Einstein developed a theory about space?

It was about time, too!

What did the alien robot say to the fuel pump?

Take your finger out of your ear when I'm talking to you!

What do you call a
noisy spaceship?

A space racket!

What do you call a
really scary alien?

An extra-terror-estrial!

Where do aliens go to study?

VERY high school!

How do you get a robot to come to a party?

Send it a tin-vitation!

Why doesn't the Sun need to go to college?

Because it has a million degrees!

What does Jupiter use to hold up his jeans?

An asteroid belt!

Why did the Sun go to school?

To get brighter!

What do you call a glass robot?

See-Through PO!

What do planets like to read?

Comet books.

Did you hear about the alien who wondered where the Sun went at night?

Eventually, it dawned on him!

Did you hear about the astronaut who was reading a book on antigravity?

It was impossible to put down!

What drink do aliens like best?

Gravi-tea!

What do aliens call astronauts in spaceships?

Canned food!

What do aliens call junk food?

Unidentified Frying Objects!

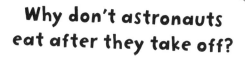

Why don't astronauts eat after they take off?

Because they've just had a big launch!

What was the sick alien's temperature?

Absolute zero!

How do you get directions in space?

Askeroid!

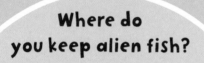

Where do you keep alien fish?

In a planetarium!

What do you call an alien wearing platform heels?

A Shoe-FO!

First alien: Do you like people?

Second alien: Yes, but I can only eat a few at a time.

Where can you leave your spaceship when visiting a planet?

At a parking meteor!

Why did the astronaut cover his spaceship in mustard?

So the aliens couldn't ketchup with him!

Why didn't the Dog Star laugh at the joke?

It was too Sirius!

Which dance does Neil Armstrong like best?

The Moon Walk!

How do you tip over a spaceship?

Rocket!

What do you call a piece of gum in space?

A Chew-FO!

What do planets sing at karaoke parties?

Nep-Tunes!

Why are meteors very good at soccer?

Because they're shooting stars!

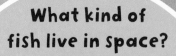

What kind of fish live in space?

Starfish!

What do you call a rodent that's gone to outer space?

A mouse-tronaut!

What do you call an alien with three eyes?

An Aliiien!

What does the Moon do when his hair gets too long?

Eclipse it!

What do aliens use to decorate their cakes?

Mars-ipan!

How do you know if there's an alien in your house?

There'll be a spaceship parked in front!

Daft Doctors

What do you call a sick crocodile?

An illigator!

Did you hear about the frog that had a breakdown?

It got toad away!

Why did the clown call the doctor?

Because he broke his funny bone!

Why did the chicken visit the doctor?

It was feeling fowl!

Why did the mummy think it had a cold?

Because of its coffin!

Why did the germ cross the microscope?

To get to the other slide!

Patient: Doctor, my nose is all red and looks like a strawberry.

Doctor: Here you go. Put this cream on it.

What's green and has four legs and a trunk?

A seasick elephant!

Did you hear about the bear that ended up in hospital?

It had a grizzly accident!

Patient: Doctor, I think I'm a bell. What should I do?

Doctor: Take this medicine, and if nothing changes, give me a ring!

Patient: Doctor, I feel like a wigwam or a tepee all the time!

Doctor: That just means you're two tents.

What did the little broom say to the big broom?

I just can't get to sweep!

Patient: Doctor, I keep thinking I'm a bridge!

Doctor: What's come over you?

Patient: One large truck and six cars!

Patient: Doctor, I keep thinking I'm a wasp!

Doctor: Buzz off, and stop bothering me!

**What should you
do if a hippo
sneezes?**

Get out of the way!

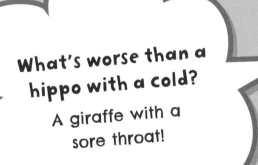

**What's worse than a
hippo with a cold?**

A giraffe with a
sore throat!

What happened when William Shakespeare visited the doctor for his cold?

The doc said it was much achoo about nothing!

Patient: Doctor, I keep eating nuts, bolts, and screws.

Doctor: That's riveting!

What do you give to an ailing citrus fruit?

Lemon-aid!

What did one elevator say to the other?

I think I'm coming down with something!

Why did the rocket visit the doctor?

To get its booster shot!

Did you hear about the pig that went on a plane?

He caught swine flu!

Patient: Doctor, I'm really afraid that I've turned into a vampire.

Doctor: Necks, please!

What's a dentist's top attraction at the amusement park?

The "fluor-ride!"

Patient: Doctor, help! I think I'm shrinking!

Doctor: Wait there, and be a little patient.

A man goes to see the doctor. He has a cucumber in one ear, a breadstick in the other ear, and a banana up his nose. The doctor knows instantly what is wrong.

"You're not eating properly!"

What do dentists call their X-rays?

Tooth pics!

My mother's a dreadful dancer. She has two left feet.

My mother's like that, too. The doctor told her to wear flip-flips.

Why did the deer visit the dentist?

He needed his buck teeth fixed!

Why did the van bounce down the road?

It was a hiccup truck!

Why did the pony visit the doctor?

It was a little horse!

Did you hear about the man who swallowed his money?

The doctor was looking for signs of change.

Why did the computer sneeze?

Because it had a virus!

What did the doctor say to the volcano?

You need to quit smoking!

A sheep went to see the vet. "I feel like I always have a cloud hanging over me!"

"Ah," said the vet. "It's because you're always under the weather."

Doctor, my feet smell and my nose runs. What should I do? Stand on your head!

Why did the ninja spend a week in bed?

He had kung flu!

What noise did the train make when it had a cold?

Aaaa-choo-choo!

What did one toilet say to the other toilet?

You look flushed!